Chocolate

Riches from the Rainforest

by Robert Burleigh

Harry N. Abrams, Inc., Publishers
In association with The Field Museum, Chicago

From chocolate
chickens to chocolate
milk, from chocolate
chunks to the most
elegant candies
carefully brushed
to look their best,
there is a perfect
chocolate for everyone.
The robbers in this
1920s ad for Fry's
cocoa seem happy
with their haul!

Chocolate. It is that dark, pleasantly bittersweet, creamy, luscious, mouthwatering, impossible-to-forget taste. *Mmmmm.*

Chocolate. Hot chocolate on a cold night, chocolate cake topped with chocolate ice cream at a birthday party, or chocolate chip cookies plucked from the cookie jar before bed. *Chocolate.* Chocolate milk, chocolate brownies, chocolate fudge, chocolate pudding, chocolate cheesecake, and chocolate candy bars . . .

It is not surprising that there are so many chocolate goodies—most people in our country say chocolate is their favorite flavor. What is *really* surprising is the story of chocolate itself.

Where does chocolate come from?

How is it made? Did Columbus discover it? Did Thomas Edison invent it? Did someone just find it growing somewhere, ready to eat?

The truth is even stranger: All the chocolate you eat comes from the seeds of one kind of tree. The seeds, of course, go through many changes on the way to your candy bar. But it all starts in the tropical rainforests of the world.

These rainforests are found near the equator. They are warm and humid and filled with exotic birds, animals, flowers, and trees. And one of those trees is the source of all chocolate—the cacao (ca-COW) tree.

Cacao. *Kakawa.* The name was first used 3,000 years ago, when a people called the Olmecs inhabited what is now Mexico. Perhaps while wandering through the dense undergrowth, the Olmecs came upon a tree with small, five-petaled white flowers and oddly shaped pods. And so the chocolate story begins.

Cacao trees often grow near a "mother" tree. The larger tree shades the young tree as it develops.

The cacao tree, reaching a height of thirty feet or more, grows under the sheltering shade, or canopy, of the taller trees around it. Its flowers, which are pollinated by a gnatlike fly called a midge, bloom throughout the year. But that is only the beginning.

What comes next is perhaps the strangest thing about the cacao's appearance. Dozens of oval-shaped, foot-long pods, which change color from green to yellow to purple-red as they ripen, grow from all parts of the tree, even the trunk. From the trunk? Early European drawings of the cacao tree, showing the pods growing from the trunk, were thought by many to be just bad illustrations. But it is true. Imagine a tree dotted with many colorful footballs!

Split the pod open and look inside. It is filled with a thick whitish pulp. Dig deeper still. Stacked in columns in the center of the pulp (which is delicious but has no taste of chocolate) are rows of pale, almond-sized seeds. And it is these cacao-tree seeds—after they are fermented, dried, roasted, shelled, and crushed to a smooth paste—from which chocolate is made.

Inside the pod, almond-sized seeds nestle in white pulp.

Cacao trees have small white flowers that are pollinated by tiny midges.

Oval, football-sized cacao pods are green and unripe now. As they ripen, bright colors will blaze forth.

Who figured it out?

Who figured this out? No one knows. If it was the Olmecs who first broke open the pods, it was probably not for the seeds—which are extremely bitter until they are treated—but for the sweet-tasting pulp. In fact, people in Brazil and other parts of South America still make a drink from this pulp.

The earliest clear record of humans consuming chocolate comes later, around 1,500 years ago. The Maya, who lived in the same region as the earlier Olmecs, built a great civilization that included huge temples, hieroglyphics (picture writing), accurate calendars—and a passion for chocolate.

From the remains of their art and hieroglyphics, we know that the Maya held chocolate in the highest esteem. In religious celebrations, the Maya even offered chocolate to their gods. We also know how the Maya made chocolate and who among them consumed it. Chocolate pots with painted pictures of the cacao tree have been found in burial sites. Some of the pots even contain traces of chocolate!

Instead of eating it, the Maya *drank* their chocolate from these pots. In fact, the Maya—and all chocolate users up to very recent times—only drank chocolate. Until the mid-1800s, chocolate did not even exist as a solid food.

Some parts of the chocolate-making process have changed little over the centuries. The Maya separated the seeds from the pulp, then put them in a warm, dark place to ferment. (Fermentation, decay caused by time and natural chemicals, creates changes in flavor.) They dried the seeds in the sun. And they roasted them on a stone griddle.

The Maya used this ceramic griddle to toast cacao seeds.

Metates like this one have been used to grind cacao seeds for hundreds of years.

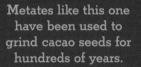

This clay statue, decorated with cacao seeds, was discovered in an ancient Maya house.

Chocolate residue, 1,500 years old, still clings to the inside of this Maya pot. It is decorated with the hieroglyphic for *kakawa*— that is, cacao.

A Maya king is offered a drink of chocolate— but he seems to be full.

The whole process takes about two weeks. During that time, two things happen. First, the seeds turn brown. Second, and more important, they begin to take on the flavor of chocolate.

After removing the shells, the Maya crushed the roasted seeds into a thick paste on a curved grinding stone called a metate. When the paste hardened, small chunks were broken off, mixed into water, and carefully poured back and forth between two pots.

The back-and-forth pouring was important to help mix the fatty part of the seed with the chocolate part of the seed. (Indeed, the seed's fat may have been a useful addition to the Maya diet.) The pouring—the Maya held the two pots several feet apart, one above the other—also formed a bubbly foam on the top of the liquid. And it was this rich chocolaty foam that the Maya loved.

Not, however, *all* the Maya. At first many Maya drank chocolate. But later the Maya came to consider chocolate so important that only the wealthy nobles and warriors who ruled the empire could drink it. This is another "chocolate tradition" that lasted for many centuries: Chocolate was a drink consumed only by the powerful and the rich.

Planting cacao trees and harvesting the seeds is hard work. Maybe the Maya peasants who performed that work

Incense burners are still used by descendants of the ancient Maya to make offerings of cacao.

occasionally stole a few of the cacao seeds and sampled the king's beverage.

Certainly that early chocolate was not a drink we would savor today. At that time, there was no sugar in the Americas. Chocolate was sweetened (if at all) with honey. Often the Maya added special flavorings to their chocolate. Chili peppers—hot and not so hot—were one favorite. Others included crushed flower petals and vanilla. But these flavors were less to soften the bitter chocolate taste than to add a spicy difference to it, the way someone today might add a few strawberries to a dish of chocolate ice cream.

The Maya could be called the world's first chocolatiers.

(Chocolatier is a modern word used to describe anyone skilled at making chocolate dishes.) But they were only one in a long line of peoples who played a part in chocolate's story.

In Maya temples, chocolate was served to kings and priests.

The Aztecs, who rose to power around 1200 A.D., followed in the Maya's footsteps. The Aztecs ruled over a wide empire centered in Tenochtitlán (ten-notch-teet-LAHN), located in what is today Mexico City. But unlike the Maya, the Aztecs did not grow cacao trees themselves. Because their lands lay outside of—but close to—the rainforests of Central America, they traded for the cacao seeds. Or else they demanded the seeds as payment from the people they conquered.

Merchants traveled to and from Tenochtitlán. Some of them, hauling loads of cacao seeds, exchanged them for other goods. In time the seeds became a kind of money, so that for a few centuries in the Central American region, money really *did* grow on trees. (Today people in Ecuador still call cacao seeds *pepe de oro,* or "seeds of gold"—just as the Spanish at one time called the cacao pods *oro negro,* or "black gold.")

People paid for many goods with cacao seeds. A turkey, for example, was worth a hundred seeds. A small rabbit was worth thirty. And a certain tiny salamander (an Aztec delicacy!) was worth four. Some shrewd traders even made fake cacao seeds, placing real seeds at the top of their sacks—and at the bottom, shells filled with dirt.

Just as the Maya had offered chocolate to their gods, the Aztecs offered their chocolate drink to their god Quetzalcoatl (ket-sal-ko-AT-l). As part of their religion, the Aztecs sacrificed humans to their gods. The victims were often given a special drink before going to their deaths.

The special drink was chocolate- mixed with blood.

Like the Maya, the Aztecs added spices to their chocolate. Sometimes they added cornmeal, and other times crushed achiote (ah-chee-OH-tay), the seed of the annatto tree, to give the drink the color of blood.

The Aztecs prized their chocolate (which they drank hot rather than cold), especially when it had a strong flavor. Whatever the taste, they consumed lots of it. In the palace of Montezuma II, the last Aztec emperor, the ruler and his many guards and servants were said to drink about 2,000 pots of chocolate a day.

Montezuma's cacao seed "bank" was impressive, too. One Spanish writer said that the emperor's cacao warehouse contained 960 million seeds. That would be enough seeds to make more than 25 million of today's chocolate bars! But Montezuma's empire was not destined to last.

Offerings of cacao were made to the Aztec god Quetzalcoatl.

Aztecs drank their chocolate out of this vessel and many, many more like it.

Early Mexicans prepare and serve their favorite drink in this 1620 Spanish engraving.

At tax time, Aztecs paid with cacao seeds or other goods. This sixteenth-century document shows some possiblities: to the left of the jaguar pelt are a gourd used for drinking chocolate and a bag of cacao seeds.

Tenochtitlán, the Aztec capital, was a big city in the early 1500s, with tall buildings, bridges, and canals.

The Aztec world—and the history of chocolate—underwent great changes soon after Christopher Columbus first reached the Americas in 1492. Columbus was followed by various groups of Spanish soldiers, called conquistadors (kon-KEES-ta-doors). The conquistadors were searching for gold, not exotic foods. At first, they gave chocolate mixed reviews. Hernando Cortés, leader of the Spanish army that defeated the Aztecs, called it "the divine drink which fights fatigue." On the other hand, a less enthusiastic Spaniard reported that chocolate "seems more a drink for pigs than for humanity."

Hernando Cortés led the Spanish forces that conquered the Aztec empire. He called chocolate "the divine drink which builds up resistance and fights fatigue."

Chocolate was bitter, harsh, and hot to the tongue. So what made the Spanish—and later, other Europeans—change their minds? In a word: sugar. Sugar, remember, did not grow in the Americas. But by adding sugar to the crushed cacao seeds and mixing both with water, the Spaniards created a drink everyone could love. All across Spain, the sweetened chocolate drink became the rage. Chocolate had found a new life far from its first home.

A new name helped increase the popularity of chocolate in Spain, too. At first people hesitated to try a dark brown drink called *cacahuatl*—the Aztec word. (In Spanish, *caca* means the same thing as it does in American slang.) The word chocolate probably comes from *chocolatl,* a Spanish combination of the Maya word for "hot water" and the Aztec word for "bitter water."

The conquest of
Tenochtitlán by
Cortés's army, as
shown by a Spanish
artist in the 1500s.

The Spaniards loved chocolate. They drank their chocolate both heated and chilled. They liked to dip bread in it, too. They also invented a utensil called a *molinillo,* a wooden stick with disks at one end, which they used to spin the chocolate into a foam. Along with the *molinillo,* rich Spaniards (and later the French, Italians, and English) owned elegantly designed chocolate pots. They even used special chocolate cups whose saucers had curled edges to protect fine clothes from spills.

For a few decades, the rest of Europe was unaware of the new Spanish drink. (Some of Spain's first chocolate makers were monks, hidden away in monasteries.) In fact, during the 1500s, English and Dutch pirates, looking for gold aboard captured Spanish galleons, often found sacks of the bitter seeds—and dumped them into the sea.

But at last chocolate spread to the rest of Europe, where it became even more popular. A Spanish princess is said to have brought chocolate from Spain to France around 1630. She trumpeted her devotion to the new drink by saying: "Chocolate and the king are my

A good *molinillo* was needed for frothy chocolate.

Spanish monks first added sugar to chocolate. Presto! A treat everyone could love. Is this pretty French woman dressed as a monk to get more chocolate?

This noblewoman's maid offers a choice: a love letter—or a cup of chocolate?

Chocolate houses were the stylish places to see and be seen in the 1600s.

Doctors often prescribed the drink as a cure for depression. Others believed that chocolate made one fat and drowsy. One 1660s verse, obviously written by a health-conscious poet, proclaimed:

Cups of chocolate,
Aye, or tea,
Are not medicines
Made for me.

Soon "chocolate houses"—meeting places for drinking chocolate or coffee and arguing about politics—arose in England. A famous English writer, Samuel Pepys, made an entry in his diary in 1664: "To a coffee house, to drink jocolatte, very good." Wealthy Englishmen met to discuss issues of the day and, often, gamble—sometimes on small, silly things. One chocolate-sipping lord lost a small fortune betting on which of two raindrops would reach the bottom of a windowpane first!

In 1753, the famous Swedish naturalist Linnaeus (li-NAY-us) gave the cacao tree its official scientific name. He named the chocolate tree *Theobroma cacao*. *Theobroma* (in Greek) means "food of the gods."

only passions." Europeans invented many ways to flavor their new drink, too. They added orange water, cinnamon, nutmeg, or cloves.

Some people also tried adding a very special "flavor"—poison! Because of chocolate's strong taste, a few people used it to disguise the equally strong taste of poisons. It was even rumored that one bishop in Mexico was poisoned with a chocolate drink after he tried to keep his flock from drinking chocolate during church services.

Debates arose, just as they do today, about chocolate's effects on health. Some people even said that drinking chocolate caused a person to fall in love.

Chocolate conquered Europe—or at least those Europeans who could pay for it.

(Along with sugar, chocolate remained very expensive.) It was still served only as a drink—and a drink for the upper classes alone. In this respect, chocolate's history had not altered from the days of the Maya and Aztecs.

Then, commoners who would never taste chocolate planted the trees and harvested the seeds from which the drink was made. Now, African slaves working in the cacao and sugar fields of the New World did the same. Sugar had earlier come to Europe from Asia, but by the 1700s it was a major New World crop, one closely connected with the slave trade. Hundreds of thousands of Africans were kidnapped and sent to the Americas to live and die on sugar and cacao plantations. Many of these plantations were on Caribbean islands, while others were in Central and South America, in the region where the cacao trees grew. (It's hard—and frightening—to believe, but even today there are reports that some cacao farms in Africa depend on forced labor to produce their crops.)

The enslaved people—whose lives seemed cheap and whose work never ended—were the main source of labor on these plantations. While aristocratic Europeans and some American colonists drank chocolate and became wealthy at the same time, the slaves labored for no wages at all. Experts today have calculated that **it took six days of a slave's life to produce one teaspoon of sugar.**

Countless hours of work go into producing the world's chocolate.

While the wealthy and fashionable sipped their chocolate . . .

. . . hundreds of thousands of Africans were kidnapped, shipped to the Americas, and forced to work as slaves on cacao and other plantations.

For 2,000 years, chocolate was a drink only for royalty and the rich, its production completely dependent on the labor of slaves and servants. How is it that today anyone can buy a chocolate bar—for less than a dollar—just about anywhere?

What changed?

One invention, more than any other, affected the way we make modern chocolate. In 1828 a Dutch inventor named Coenraad Van Houten built a press that could separate the shelled, crushed cacao seeds (known as chocolate liquor) into their two distinct parts: a fatty part and a purer chocolate part.

Remember that earlier people poured or rapidly stirred their chocolate drink to mix the fatty part of the seed with the chocolate part. When this mixing was not done well, the chocolate drink tasted, as one English-man said around 1800, "as thick as soup, and as **greasy as a fish-fryer's thumb.**" Van Houten's press forced the fat part of the seeds (called cocoa butter) from the pure chocolate part. This left small cakes of hard, dry, bitter chocolate. A revolution in chocolate had begun.

Now chocolate makers could mold candy bars by mixing the chocolate liquor with smaller portions of cocoa butter and sugar. The resulting chocolate was firm but still in a somewhat liquid state. (Cocoa butter does

Pressed chocolate is used to make cocoa powder and other products.

not melt at room temperature. Instead, it keeps the chocolate bar solid—**until it melts in your mouth.**)
The first edible solid chocolate candy finally appeared in England in 1847.

The hard cakes of pure chocolate turn into something else. Crumbled, then finely crushed, they became cocoa powder, just like the cocoa powder that is used to make the chocolate drinks we sip today.

The next advance in chocolate making took place in Switzerland. A chocolate maker named Daniel Peter discovered a way to make a lighter kind of chocolate by adding evaporated milk to the mix of chocolate liquor, cocoa butter, and sugar. The evaporated milk was made from a recipe by Henri Nestlé, an important name in chocolate to this day. The result was called "milk" chocolate, which is the sweet chocolate found in many candy bars today. (Peter first tried mixing chocolate with **cheese** rather than milk. Apparently that product was completely unsuccessful.)

Other nineteenth-century inventions improved the quality and the appearance of chocolate. One innovation, called a conching machine because it was shaped like a large seashell, rocked and rolled the liquid chocolate back and forth until even the tiniest grains of cocoa disappeared. Before this, solid chocolate had a gritty texture. After conching it was smoother than ever.

The Hershey plant was already gigantic in 1915.

Early packaging protected a favorite treat.

Another new process in the art of chocolate making was called tempering. Tempered chocolate is heated to a high temperature (higher than 150°F) and then slowly cooled. This kept the cocoa butter in the chocolate from crystallizing. Before tempering, chocolate often had a streaky, unappetizing look.

But the growing numbers of chocolate lovers still had reason to be wary. True, chocolate was cheaper and easier to buy. Now, however, fake chocolate began to appear on the English market. One study in the mid-nineteenth century found that some "chocolate" had been mixed with potato grains and colored with ground-up bricks!

In the 1890s, an American candy maker, Milton Hershey, began to bring chocolate to the public in a large-scale way. Sometimes called "the Henry Ford of chocolate" after the man who first mass-produced automobiles, Hershey got the idea for a simple chocolate bar after watching some children lick the chocolate coating off pieces of caramel candy—and throw the caramel away!

"Caramels are only a fad. Chocolate is a permanent thing," Hershey proclaimed. And he soon began to prove it. His company started turning out hundreds of thousands of bars of milk chocolate that most working people could—and did—buy.

Another important invention in the history of chocolate was the refrigerator. Refrigerators only became available to American businesses after 1900. With refrigeration, people could make and sell chocolate all year round without fearing that it would melt.

Chocolate is here to stay!

Milton Hershey

World War I (1914–1918) gave chocolate a boost, too. American troops were given chocolate as a quick-energy food. They liked what they tasted. When the war ended and the troops came home, ex-soldiers added their voices to the increased demand for chocolate. In the 1920s, many American towns had candy shops where the owners made their own chocolate candies. Hot chocolate was combined with ice cream for the first time, to produce hot fudge sundaes—even though one writer of the time protested: "Cover ice cream with hot chocolate? Ridiculous!"

Many new chocolate candies and candy bars were invented—more than 30,000 different kinds during the first decades of the twentieth century. The great majority of them came and went. Some, however, grew popular—and are still popular today. They include Hershey's Kisses, Baby Ruth, Milky Way, M&M's, and Reese's Peanut Butter Cups.

Chocolate was promoted once again as **a health food.** Ads told buyers that eating chocolate was a good way to get more milk into a child's diet or to give one an increased zest for life. Critics struck back by warning chocolate eaters that they risked tooth decay, acne, and weight gain. (The truth seems to be that chocolate by itself—in moderate quantities—does not do any harm. Of course, it is almost always accompanied by sugar, which may have undesirable effects.)

Chocolate makers also stressed the idea of giving chocolate as **a special gift.** Is chocolate a love potion, as some ancient people believed? Probably not, but Americans still spend more than $1 billion on candy (much of it chocolate) **for their valentines** every February 14.

A young man takes a cocoa break in an English shop before 1900.

Easter became a favorite chocolate holiday, full of chocolate eggs and chocolate bunnies.

France and Germany were liberated after World War II. American soldiers handed out their chocolate rations to the people to help celebrate.

In about 1950, this English exhibit showed that "the average boy during his schooldays eats this amount of chocolates and sweets!"

E AVERAGE BOY
g his SCHOOLDAYS
S THIS AMOUNT
F CHOCOLATES
ND SWEETS!

Every candy shop had its specialties— and its special fans.

Kids settle down in front of the TV for a show and a snack.

Everyone enjoys chocolate.

In some ways, modern chocolate making is very new.

Yet in other ways, it is very old. Cacao trees still grow in tropical rainforests. Central America, however, is no longer the starting point for most of the world's chocolate. Today most cacao trees grow in West Africa. One West African nation, Ivory Coast, produces a million tons of cacao seeds each year.

Unfortunately, the cacao tree is also a factor in the depletion of the world's rainforests. Often the forests are cleared to make way for cacao production. At other times, diseased cacao trees (and more than 30 percent of cacao trees die of plant diseases) are simply cut down and left in huge open spaces, again leaving the rainforest treeless and bare.

When cacao trees are removed due to disease, acres of rainforest can be destroyed.

Workers sort
the pods.

But whether the cacao tree grows in Africa, Asia, or
the Americas, the first steps in the journey that leads
to your candy bar are **the same** as
they were 1,000 years ago.

A basket of
colorful harvested
cacao pods.

The plantation workers collect
the pods, split them open
(machete-wielding pod cutters
can slice 500 pods an hour!),
store the seeds in the dark
to ferment, and set them in
the sun to dry. Just as it did
centuries ago, this part of
the process goes on for about
two weeks.

From here, though, everything changes. Workers
ship the bagged seeds to factories around the world.
An array of high-tech equipment replaces the ancient,
slow methods of making the chocolate by hand.

Rows of giant silos alongside chocolate factories
hold tons of cacao seeds. Milk from 50,000 or more
cows is delivered to some large chocolate-making
plants each day. Fast-moving machines perform all
the processes leading to the final chocolate product:
roasting, shelling, conching, and tempering.

Chocolate is often made in one factory and then shipped as a liquid (in large tanker trucks) to smaller companies, where the chocolate is poured into molds for candy bars or used to make other kinds of confections. Factories turn out **thousands of candy bars and treats every hour.** The many Tootsie Roll factories around the world, for example, manufacture a total of 49 million wrapped candies each day.

To make chocolate chips, liquid chocolate goes into a large machine. The chocolate pours down, filling chip-sized holes in a specially designed rack below the machine. The chip-filled rack moves along the assembly line, the chocolate slowly solidifying, as another rack takes its place. This rack fills,

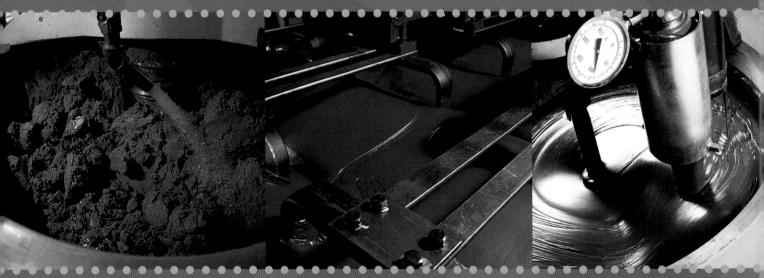

 On a cacao plantation, pods are harvested. The pods are cut open, and the seeds are removed and allowed to ferment.

3 Other ingredients, such as cocoa butter and sugar, are added to the chocolate liquor. Then the chocolate is conched (to make it smooth) and tempered (to give it a glossy sheen).

too, and moves on. In just one minute, the machine makes more than 58,000 chips! In an hour, 3.5 million chips roll down the line. **Has once-royal chocolate become completely democratic?** Not quite. At the same time that factories turn out chocolate bars and cookies by the millions, other chocolate makers are producing rich-tasting, high-priced chocolate confections. Their makers work hard to create chocolate that is creamier and more luxurious than any chocolate in your local store.

2 After fermentation, the seeds are spread to dry, then shipped to chocolate-making factories around the world. The seeds are roasted, shelled, and crushed into a paste called chocolate liquor.

4 Each day, thousands of pounds of chocolate, attended by thousands of workers, flow down production lines to become the chocolate candies we love.

Can you imagine
wearing chocolate
clothing, or eating a
chocolate bug?
Chocolate comes in
every shape, size,
and color, and
making it is an art.

Special cooking schools teach students how to make unusual chocolate dishes. Chocolate theme parks have sprung up in the United States and Great Britain. Teams of chocolate makers compete for prizes around the world. And there are even chocolate artists who will make your heart's desire, whether you want a chocolate toy train or a full-size chocolate car!

Most people call chocolate their favorite flavor. What is it about chocolate that so many people love? Describing the taste of chocolate is not easy. Is it sweet? Is it bitter? Is it sweet and sour? Is it thick? Is it thin? Does it arrive with a sharp burst or leave with a lingering caress?

We know that chocolate is high in carbohydrates. This makes it a quick, high-energy food. Cortés was on to something when he said the Aztec chocolate drink helped fight fatigue. The first explorers who reached the North Pole drank almost nothing but cocoa on the way. U.S. soldiers in World War II, like those in World War I, were issued special chocolate bars as survival rations. And chocolate was even taken as a ration by the American astronauts who landed on the moon!

A love potion. A high-energy snack. The "food of the gods." But maybe there's something simpler still. Experts say that chocolate contains nearly 300 different flavors. Perhaps, to the person about to bite into a banana split with double hot fudge topping, this is really the secret of its charm. Maybe, if so many flavors are hiding in it—

chocolate has a little something for everyone!

glossary

Bittersweet chocolate Chocolate made with more cocoa solids and less sugar than semisweet or milk chocolate. It has a deep, strong, slightly sweet flavor.

Carbohydrates Nutrients that are the body's main source of energy.

Central America The region running from central Mexico to Panama. During the pre-Spanish period (before approximately 1500), many groups of people flourished in this region, and together they were responsible for the development of chocolate. Some of the major groups of people were (in chronological order) the Olmecs, the Maya, and the Aztecs, whose great capital city, Tenochtitlán, was located in what is today Mexico City.

Chocolate liquor The dark nonalcoholic paste produced by grinding the nib (the shelled cacao seed) to a smooth, liquid state. Chocolate liquor is the basis of all chocolate.

Chocolatier A professional who specializes in making fine-quality chocolate and chocolate confections.

Cocoa butter The fat found in cacao seeds. About one-half of the cacao seed consists of fat, and this fat, when not used in the making of candy bars, is often used in the production of cosmetics.

Cocoa cake The dry, solid cake produced by extracting the cocoa butter from chocolate liquor. Cocoa cakes are crushed and sifted to produce cocoa powder.

Conching A process by which liquid chocolate is further mixed to give it an even smoother, creamier texture.

Confection A specially prepared sweet candy, often dipped in or covered with chocolate.

Evaporated milk Milk that has been concentrated by removing some of the water.

Fermentation A decaying process that alters the chemistry and flavor of organic substances.

Metate The curved stone slab used by the Maya and Aztecs to grind shelled cacao seeds to a paste.

Midge The gnatlike fly that pollinates the cacao flower. The midge is said to possess the fastest wing beat in the insect world—around 1,000 beats per second!

Milk chocolate A mixture of chocolate liquor, cocoa butter, milk, sugar, and other flavorings. Milk chocolate is the sweetest of the chocolates, containing around 50 percent sugar. It is used in the making of many desserts and candy bars.

Molinillo A long-handled wooden utensil used by the Spanish and, later, the French for stirring chocolate drinks.

Montezuma II (also known as Cuauhtémoc) The Aztec ruler who first welcomed the Spanish conquistador Hernando Cortés in 1519. Montezuma, a great lover of chocolate, was later murdered by the Spanish and his empire overthrown in 1521.

Rainforest A dense forest, often though not always found in a tropical region, with an annual rainfall of at least 100 inches.

Semisweet chocolate Chocolate that contains slightly more sugar than bittersweet chocolate and less sugar than milk chocolate.

Shell The hard outer coating of a seed. Cacao shells are used as cattle feed and even as mulch for gardens, where they often give the garden a slight chocolate aroma.

Slave trade The transportation of black Africans to colonial regions of the world for sale as slaves. The slave trade was part of a triangular trading system in which sugar, cacao, and other goods produced by enslaved people were shipped from America to Europe, while guns and other goods were shipped from Europe to Africa to capture more potential slaves. Profits were made at all points by those who controlled the slave trade.

Tempering A process of heating and cooling liquid chocolate that gives it a shiny, even appearance, free of gray streaks and dots.

White chocolate A mixture of sugar, cocoa butter, milk, and flavorings. However, since chocolate liquor is not part of the blend, white chocolate is technically not chocolate at all.

Author's Note

When I began the research that led to this book, I knew only one thing: I love chocolate! Most people do. But like many others, I knew little about chocolate's long history and even less about how chocolate gets into the cakes and candy bars I devour so happily.

Fortunately, I had a good guide in my chocolate studies. *Chocolate: Riches from the Rainforest* was written in association with The Field Museum, Chicago. The knowledgeable Field Museum researchers, and the resources they pointed me to, opened up a wide, complex, intriguing world of chocolate.

Chocolate's story is linked with the highs and the lows of the human condition during the past two millennia. Today, chocolate is easy to find and inexpensive to buy. But growing cacao and producing edible chocolate has always meant a great deal of work, work that was almost invariably done by the poorest laborers. Even before Africans were kidnapped and brought to the Americas to work on cacao plantations, Maya and Aztec rulers used peasant workers to make their chocolate. Tragically, allegations of slavelike working conditions on some African cacao plantations continue today.

Slowly, industrialization and democracy have brought chocolate to more and more people. Starting in the early nineteenth century, chocolate makers found ways to convert what had formerly been only a drink into a solid food. The chocolate candy bar was born—and the rest is history. Today, the average American eats around twelve pounds of chocolate each year!

More chocolate, tastier chocolate, more chocolaty chocolate . . . chocolate lovers are always finding new ways to enjoy this favorite. Why is chocolate so alluring? Experts still aren't sure. So perhaps there is nothing to do but savor the taste as well as understand the complicated process that has gone into producing this luscious food, truly a gift from the rainforest. I sincerely hope that this book helps the reader do both of these things.

I am grateful for the support of The Field Museum staff, and particularly for the help of Anamari Golf. I am equally indebted to my editor, Laaren Brown, who carefully guided the manuscript through its various changes. And finally, many thanks to my wife, Jenny Roberts, who for long, long hours listened to and read my thoughts on this subject—without once losing her taste for chocolate!

—*Robert Burleigh*

The Field Museum CHICAGO

The exhibition *Chocolate* and its national tour were developed by The Field Museum, Chicago, and were supported, in part, by the National Science Foundation.

Bibliography

*Ammon, Richard. *The Kids' Book of Chocolate*. Atheneum, 1987.
Bloom, Carol. *All About Chocolate*. Macmillan, 1998.
*Boynton, Sandra. *Chocolate: The Consuming Passion*. Workman Publishing, 1982.
Brenner, Joel Glenn. *The Emperors of Chocolate*. Random House, 1999.
*Burford, Betty. *Chocolate by Hershey*. Carolrhoda Books, Inc., 1994.
*Busenberg, Bonnie. *Vanilla, Chocolate & Strawberry*. Lerner Publications Company, 1994.
Coe, Sophie D. and Michael D. *The True History of Chocolate*. Thames & Hudson Ltd., 1996.
*Dahl, Roald. *Charlie and the Chocolate Factory*. Knopf, 1964.
*Jaspersohn, William. *Cookies*. Macmillan, 1993.

*Easier reading for younger readers

Photo credits

(L = left, R = right): Front and back endpapers, © Catherine Ursillo/Photo Researchers; 4 L bottom, © M. & E. Bernheim/Woodfin Camp & Associates; R middle, © Jeremy Horner/Panos Pictures; 5 L middle, © David Madison/Bruce Coleman, Inc.; 6 L top, © Olivia Baumgartner/Corbis Sygma; L bottom, © Jim LeGoy/Getty Images; top middle, © Bill Debold/Getty Images; R top center, © Jim LeGoy/Getty Images; 7 L top, © Michel Setboun/Corbis Sygma; R middle, Mary Evans Picture Library; 8 L, © Teresa Murray/The Field Museum; R top, © Jeremy Horner/Panos Pictures; 9 L bottom, © Kjell B. Sandved/Photo Researchers; R top, © Frans Lanting/Minden Pictures; R bottom, © Paul Fridman/Corbis Sygma; 11 L top, © 2001 The Field Museum/J. Weinstein A114058_2c; L middle, © 2001 The Field Museum/J. Weinstein A114059_2c; bottom, © Justin Kerr; R top © George F. Mobley/NGS Picture Collection; R middle, National Archaeological Museum of Guatemala; 12 L, © 2001 The Field Museum/J. Weinstein A114060_2c; 13 R, © Malcolm Kirk/Peter Arnold, Inc.; 15 L, © Bodelian Library/Oxford University; R top, Newberry Library, Chicago; R middle top, American Museum of Natural History/Photo by John Taylor Bigelow; R middle bottom, Mary Evans Picture Library; R bottom, © Robert Frerck/Odyssey, Chicago; 16 R, National Museum of History, Spain/Giraudon/Art Resource, NY; 17 British Embassy, Mexico City/The Bridgeman Art Library; 18 L middle, "Louise-Anne de Bourbon, Mlle de Charolais" by Charles Natoire/Chateaux de Versailles et de Trianon, France/Art Resource, NY; R middle, Mary Evans Picture Library; 19 L top, British Museum, London; 20 © Mary Baber/Olsson-Baber Photography; 21 top, "The Penthievre Family" by Jean Baptist/Chateau de Versailles, France/The Bridgeman Art Library; bottom, Mary Evans Picture Library; 22-23 © Mary Baber/Olsson-Baber Photography; 24 top, Hershey Community Archives; 25 L, Hershey Community Archives; 26 R middle, Corbis; R bottom, Hulton Archive by Getty Images; 27 L top, Corbis; all others, Hulton Archive by Getty Images; 28 bottom, © Tony Dallios/Panos Pictures; 29 L top, Getty Images; L middle, © Jeremy Horner/Panos Pictures; 30 L middle, © Victor Englebert; L bottom, © Michel Setboun/Corbis Sygma; middle middle, © Mary Baber/Olsson-Baber Photography; middle bottom, © John Ficara/Woodfin Camp & Associates; R middle, Commodity Organic Products, Inc.; R bottom, Peter's Chocolate; 31 L middle, © M. & E. Bernheim/Woodfin Camp & Associates; L bottom, © Michel Setboun/Corbis Sygma; middle bottom, PhotoDisc; middle bottom, © Richard Nowitz; R middle, © Lester Sloan/Woodfin Camp & Associates; R bottom, © Sepp Seitz/Woodfin Camp & Associates; 32 L bottom, © Manfred Selow/Corbis Sygma; R top, © Michel Setboun/Corbis Sygma; R middle, © Julien Hekiman/Corbis Sygma; 33 L top, © Catherine Ursillo/Photo Researchers; 36 L top, © Jaime Biondo. Jacket: Background, FoodPix; front R top, © Jeremy Horner/Panos Pictures; front R bottom, © Paul Fridman/Corbis Sygma; back middle, Newberry Library, Chicago; front flap, © Teresa Murray/The Field Museum; back flap, © M. & E. Bernheim/Woodfin Camp & Associates.

Book design: Jelly Associates NYC

Library of Congress Cataloging-in-Publication Data
Burleigh, Robert.
Chocolate: riches from the rainforest / By Robert Burleigh.
p. cm.
Includes bibliographical references.
Summary: Traces the history of chocolate from a drink of the Olmec and Maya and later in Europe to its popularity around the world today.
ISBN 0-8109-5734-5
1. Cookery (Chocolate)—Juvenile literature. 2. Chocolate—Juvenile literature. [1. Chocolate.] I. Title.
TX767.C5 B94 2002
641.3'374—dc21
2001003744

Hershey's Kisses® and Reese's Peanut Butter Cups® are registered trademarks of Hershey Foods Corp. M&M's® and Milky Way® are registered trademarks of Mars, Inc. Baby Ruth® is a registered trademark of Nestlé USA, Inc.

Printed and bound in Hong Kong
10 9 8 7 6 5 4 3 2 1

Harry N. Abrams, Inc.
100 Fifth Avenue
New York, N.Y. 10011
www.abramsbooks.com

Abrams is a subsidiary of

LA MARTINIÈRE
GROUPE